A SKEIN OF TIME

ZANZARA HENNIGAN

Religious Research Press
Post Office Box 208
Grand Island, Florida 32735

Dedicated to
Franklin Loehr, D.D.
and Dr. John Christopher Daniels

Cover Design by Adele Lewis
Word Processing by Carol Castle

A SKEIN OF TIME

ISBN 0-9681765-1-8

Printed in Canada

INTRODUCTION

Church of Religious Research has a specialized ministry in research and publication chiefly regarding the nature and purposes, the problems and opportunities of the soul as it incarnates in a physical body.

The research conducted by our Founder, Franklin Loehr, D.D. included recognition of the ability to contact spiritual realms, and testing the validity of messages and impressions received. Through this he discovered a high spirit being, Dr. John Christopher Daniels, who made himself known, as he spoke through Franklin or Grace Wittenberger Loehr. "Dr. John" said he served Jesus the Christ by learning to read the Akashic Records (of souls) from their highest perspective, in the most accurate manner.

Our research library contains nearly 6000 life readings and teachings given by Dr. John, full of understanding about the nature of the soul, and the many lessons it has to learn through its personalities on Earth.

One basic teaching is that the soul as it is individuated out of the beingness of God is androgynous. Before incarnating, each soul is polarized into its masculine and feminine halves, with the mental and emotional attributes of each gender. The masculine half originally was given the task of physical survival; ingenuity, physical strength, some shrewdness and competitiveness were essential characteristics. The feminine half had the attributes of nurturing, values of truth, beauty and goodness, and an openness to spirit realms.

These half souls grow by means of their Earth

experiences -- usually through a total of 60-100 significant incarnations as different persons. It is essential that this growth be balanced for both the masculine and feminine halves by "learning how the other half lives." If not, these half souls will become crystallized, unable to meld with the opposite gender's beingness and grow in preparation for again functioning androgynously beyond the incarnational stage.

The usual pattern is that the first several incarnations will be in the native gender -- then 1-3 incarnations in non-native gender, then back to native gender again for several lifetimes. The early non-native gender lifetimes for young souls are full of difficult adjustments. Older souls learn to make these gender shifts smoothly and live equally well as men or women. In this way, when the whole soul reunites at the end of the reincarnational cycle, it will have grown greatly through experience in both genders by each half soul in a well-balanced way.

More information about the problems and opportunities of young souls can be found in our book Dr. John: He Can Read Your Past Lives.

In this book you will read the life story of a masculine (half) soul who has progressed well in taking mastery of earthliving as a man. But when it is required to have a feminine lifetime, the soul is strongly opposed to allowing the development of feminine beingness to balance its growth. Lorraine's life reading indicated that solving this problem was the chief purpose of her lifetime as a person. This lesson is one all souls must learn -- if not in one lifetime, then it will be repeated until it is learned.

Lorraine's mother, Zanzara her pen name, also had a life reading and has been a very interested Religious Research member for years. She wanted to share this story of her daughter whom she loved greatly. You, too, can learn from her story.

-- Isabel Pinkston and Helen Roberts, Editors --

PROLOGUE

Family trees became a popular search in the twentieth century. But an even more popular tree to come will be an original people one, when an individual's past-life relationships are charted with those entities held dear to him or her in this present earth life. A personality is here as a physical being, in a material existence, representing an immortal soul. Here we are placed in order to make spiritual growth, and often to make amends for errors made in previous relationships.

Some physicists speculate that photons may be conscious. Einstein proved that light is composed of photons. Photons, which are energy, appear to process information and to react accordingly, and they also seem to be organic. Quanta was the name given to packets of energy. The energy in each light quantum of a particular color, is the frequency of light multiplied by Planck's constant. Planck is the father of quantum mechanics.

Energy is the consciousness of the universe, and we exist here only in a three-dimensional world. There are other dimensions and it is into these other dimensions that the immortal part must travel.

Gary Zukav in The Dancing Wu Li Masters speaks of an experiment made with light going through two holes in a cardboard and being reflected at the back. The light goes through each of the two holes individually. In his language, he could run upstairs when the light shows through one, and downstairs when the light shows through the other. He leads us on to show that many dimensions can exist

1

and not be visible, since light going through both of the openings at one time has its own place, and is not consistent with the other areas.

Each of us has an aura around our bodies radiating in specific colors which often change with one's emotions. When the Kirlians were doing their experiments and the wife happened to hurt her leg, she looked at it under their apparatus, and was surprised to find only red lights being emitted. No other color was visible while the leg was giving her pain. It is quite possible that many people in past years were able to see auras. Today only a few who are gifted have that ability. But where else could the following expressions have come from: "Green with envy," "Red with rage," or even "Tickled pink!"

A very few gifted people can diagnose illness by looking at a individual's aura. Experiments have been done whereby the diagnosis, given by someone looking at a patient's aura, has been confirmed by the medical doctor. Illness is said to be visible in an aura as a muddied color long before it can be discovered in the physical body. Perhaps our future health practices will combine aura readings, along with holistic medicine, osteopathic or chiropractic manipulation, all working for the health benefit of each human being.

It was my decision quite some time ago, that the mind is located in the aura, and recent readings seem to agree with this. I believe the mind and the aura leave the physical shell at what we term death; when the golden bowl (formerly seen as a halo) shatters, and the silver cord is severed (that portion attached to the physical body and used during our dream state or when we travel in the astral).

Scientific studies have measured before and after death and found that there definitely is a slight weight loss.

Anyone planning to do astral travel would do well to read Lobsang Rampa's Chapters of Life volume. Such travel can be dangerous since there are malefic spirits waiting to come into a human body to continue a former life of carousing entities who have not gained spiritually. We are definitely here to learn and to mature spiritually. Changes have been noted after certain people dabble with drugs -- it can be a very dangerous business.

The list of books that are informative on the topics mentioned is a lengthy one. Stalking the Wild Pendulum by Itshak Bentov discusses the mechanics of consciousness. The Tao of Physics by Fritjof Capra is an earlier written view of human consciousness.

According to information from the Church of Religious Research, Inc. souls are grouped in Cosmic Families of about 50 members, with old souls moving on, and young souls being added. Usually we as persons incarnate with one or more of our Cosmic Family in a close family-or-friend tie. Older family members help the younger ones through difficult times, stand by them in Love, help them grow in ability to handle earthliving and develop spiritually. Cosmic Family members are often together in different roles here or elsewhere. Sometimes other friendships are formed over different lifetimes that can become very close, even though these are not cosmic. We incarnate for different purposes in order to experience all of the lessons earthliving has for us to learn.

In our time we should see a melding of religion and science. Rev. Franklin Loehr, founder of Church of Religious Research, was one who wrote on this topic. Some of his published books were The Power of Prayer on Plants, Diary After Death and Science, Religion, and the Development of Religion as a Science.

My hope would be that I can contribute toward more peaceful relations between people through Lorraine's story. Knowing you have to make up in another life for wrongs you commit should become a deterrent to the educated. "Whatsoever a man soweth, that shall he also reap."

Zanzara
November 7, 1989

4

CHAPTER I

"What's this? Tell Lover Boy to get off his ass!" David Young looked very sheepish as he spoke these words to us, but whatever Lorraine had wanted him to say before that, he had commented, "Oh I couldn't say that," which led me to believe Lorraine had been using four letter words.

I had promised that I would go with her daughter Laverne to see David Young and we were fulfilling a promise made in August of 1985. My sister, Arlene, would not go with us but later she clarified a problem from an earlier message.

"Have Lover Boy take my ashes over to Maui, travel first class, and drink his face off!!" We knew she had wanted her ashes scattered at Makena or Big Beach, but calling Larry "Lover Boy" and the expression "drink his face off" were new to me. Arlene was familiar with them all.

PRAYER: Our Father in Heaven, we ask Thy help now as we seek to set ourselves aside and let only that which concerns Thy child, Lorraine Adams, to be brought to her from a source higher than all of us. Thou dost know her better than she knows herself, and Thy great heart dost reach out in love to her as she walks the pathway. Guide her and sustain her throughout all the days of her years with greater purpose, greater peace, fulfillment and understanding. In Jesus' name, Amen.

Thus began the life reading for Eleanor Lorraine, who was born April 23, 1939, at 6:30 a.m. at Bralorne, British Columbia. The Akashic Record reader was Dr. John Christopher Daniels; channel, Grace Wittenberger Loehr; conductor, Dr. Franklin Loehr.

Dr. Loehr: Her basic need is to know who she is and why. Why is her soul having this incarnation as Eleanor Lorraine, and what or who is her soul? There will be other questions but this is the big one.

This was answered in full as follows:

Dr. John Daniels: This is basically a masculine soul, one who is well started in earthliving and who has developed a very good degree of competence and resourcefulness in handling earthliving in masculine expression. It is a soul well started in earth experience, and well started in cosmic experience.

It is a soul who has a well-defined sense of individuality, and it prizes that individuality. It has done well in masculine personality lives, choosing its goals and drawing the given personality into co-operating with it to attain those goals. The major experiences have been within the masculine framework. The feminine framework of earth experiences is not, let us say, as agreeable to the soul.

It accepts the feminine personality beingness in the understanding that such experience is a part of earthliving. But it does not find it easy to reflect its own masculine beingness as it knows it to be in and through feminine personality expression. Nor has it discovered the art of allowing the feminine personality expression to act upon the masculine beingness.

6

Inasmuch as experience in feminine beingness represents a framework basically disliked by the soul, when it does incarnate in the feminine there is present a large quota of self-centeredness. The soul holding firmly to the reality of its basic beingness, thus finds feminine beingness as a potential attack upon it. It has, as it were, defenses up in the prospect that feminine beingness might overtake the masculine nature if the soul is not constantly on guard against such intrusion.

Now this approach of earthliving has really crippled the soul, has really handicapped the soul in its experiences of feminine living. So much of its soul energy is engaged in maintaining its fortress of masculine beingness that the effect of feminine beingness does not have the opportunity to reach the soul consciousness with its own message of what it is. We have then a pattern readable in the Akashic Records wherein the soul in masculine personality expression handles earthliving with a great deal of positive resourcefulness, with resultant positive achievements. But when the same soul experiences earthliving in feminine expression, although the feminine beingness reaches the outer physical expression, and although it, as it were, puts on a layer of becomingness upon the mental and emotional body, the masculine soul really does not take the feminine beingness into itself. It holds it apart.

The results, of course, are feminine lifetimes of turmoil, of strain, of stress. There is a very good opportunity for this pattern of feminine experience of earthliving to be ended in the person of and by the effort of the present feminine personality. Her restlessness, her discontent, her dissatisfaction, represent creative opportunities to make a change in the soul's attitude toward feminine living.

As a whole, the soul's attitude is birthed in an uncomprehending understanding of what feminine living is like. Now the present feminine personality, as she understands the experience of feminine beingness in relationship to the soul, in relationship to its immortal pattern of continuingness, can indeed provide the fuller comprehension which the soul is looking for. The present personality beingness, however, to do this is going to have to establish a starting point of recognition that there are spiritual and eternal values as purposes for living.

She is going to have to turn her attention and turn her interest into discovering and becoming knowledgeable in the awareness of such values. This is something which cannot be brought to the personality by any other person. It is something she cannot experience as a gift from someone else. It is a discovery that only she can make, and it can come into activity only by her decision that she wants to do so.

If this is not the personality's choice, the present state of confusion and unhappiness will continue, simply because there is no other person who can change it. Furthermore, this state of being will continue to manifest in continuing earthlives. There can be no surcease from it. There can be no escape in the framework of closing out one lifetime and beginning another life. Because, you see, the soul as the initiator of the life problem knows only this kind of pattern to initiate.

Now the present personality is intelligent, she is competent, she is resourceful, and she can make the difference in the pattern of feminine lives which the soul experiences if she chooses to do so.

8

Lorraine and I had a double life reading done in the seventies. In obtaining this type of reading one needed to write a little about one's self, and you could ask questions about relationships with several people. We chose some family relatives and some friends. As can be gleaned from the perusal of the information given to Lorraine, she really had quite a decision to make. At the time of her enquiry she and husband Ernest were living at Okanagan Falls with three youngsters, George, John and Laverne. Ernest had adopted the two boys and was the only father they ever knew. She apparently had met Larry shortly before we wrote for the readings and she asked about both Ernest and Larry for two of her enquiries.

But perhaps I should describe Lorraine as she was at that time. She was tall for a woman and well proportioned -- a size 38D! Her hair was kept a blonde shade and often Ernest had the job of bleaching the tresses. Dressed up she was really very attractive, a "wow," and most of her wardrobe had been "Fashioned by Laverne Laverty" according to the labels.

Lorraine had two sets of clothes for herself -- for the fat times and for the thin times. When thin she looked like Marilyn Monroe's double. But being a cook, and an excellent one at that, the fat clothes were often in vogue. Appearance meant a lot to her, the image she would present to the outside world. At home it was different. There she would relax completely in a dressing gown, and in her words "let it all hang out."

In a picture from early in 1984 when she made a trip to Paris, she is both glamorous and well-dressed. She knew the clothes she should wear, and of course the men found her attractive and sexy.

Returning to the Life Reading the Conductor asks --

9

"Is there past-life acquaintance between Lorraine and Ernest?"

Dr. John: "Yes. He is very important to her. He represents a Cosmic Family member. He represents a masculine soul who in the course of his experience in earthliving ran into some of the difficulties that the Eleanor Lorraine soul has run into in adjusting to feminine living. He made the adjustments and as a result has a great deal of patience and understanding to extend to this younger cosmic member whom he sees now going through some of the same learning experiences as were formerly his.

They were together in their most recent earthlife, which was a life in the 1800's in Hawaii. They were husband and wife in that lifetime in the same roles as the present. Their beginning relationship, the first of the marriage, was good. She as the wife rather shortly conceived and brought forth a child, and that was fine. However, a number of children came in rather rapid succession, and that personality of the Lorraine soul resented the coming of the children.

She resented the role the husband put her in as essentially the mother of his children. He referred to her more as the mother of his children than his wife. She felt herself becoming unattractive. Then a younger man came into the picture who flattered her, and as it were, gave nourishment to that portion of her feminine beingness the husband was neglecting. She deserted her husband; she deserted the children. She went to live with the younger man. He was no good. He was indolent, he was lazy, and the two of them essentially became beachcombers, living off others and not productive in any way.

In rather short order, her allure as an older woman lost its charm to the younger man. He turned to younger women and she turned to other young men. They maintained a kind of liaison but felt no particular responsibility for each other.

Q: Have Lorraine and Larry past life acquaintance?

A: Yes. He represented the young man that the 1800's personality went off with.

The Lorraine soul on the soul level, as it were, has a fixation on the Larry soul in the form of the attractive younger man in the 1800's life. He represented an escape from aging. He represented the hands standing still on the clock. Because the soul has not turned its resources to the challenges of feminine beingness, it has not discovered how to face the adult years of a feminine personality expression, except in the framework of being a young woman. It has not developed the resources for facing the experience of mature womanhood.

Among Lorraine's comments sent in preparation for her life reading, she wrote, "In looking back I have for many years thought what a waste of a life this is, and I really feel more so now. I have never been happy. Perhaps I don't know what happy means!"

Rev. Franklin Loehr was concerned about Lorraine. He felt she might be quite overwhelmed by the advice she had been given at the beginning of her reading — so much so that he included for her his private telephone number. He hoped she would keep in touch with him either by writing or phoning.

He was quite right in his concern for her, but I well remember the day she phoned me that she had left Ernest, and if she would be building up more karma that was how it would be as she could not tolerate all of the fighting any longer. Shortly after that she made an attempt to commit suicide. Fortunately that was thwarted by Larry's brother who had happened to call on her, and she was taken to the hospital. It was only a short time later that Larry left his home and each had a separate rental place in the same area. By then he was also working in the same hotel as she was, and before too many months went by they decided to move in together. Only a short time later they left Penticton and both flew to Maui where there had always been a strong pull.

The cost of living is very high on Maui and it was difficult for them to live there. They did manage to find part-time work -- Larry as a night watchman and Lorraine as a waitress. At the intercontinental she met Naomi, a friend she corresponded with later. Naomi was also a waitress at that time.

Larry and Lorraine often walked to the many beaches; they particulary liked the old site of the Keawalai'i Church. Both eventually found Makena or Oleana Beach, and were happy there near the "Black Rocks" which divided the Big Beach from the little one that is often called "Nude Beach." It was perhaps only six months later that they were back in Canada at the Sunset Marina, one doing the cooking and the other handling the bar and waiter work. Both fixed up an upstairs apartment that commanded a beautiful view of the ocean. It was fixed up too well; the owners decided to move into it and so the couple rented an apartment at Horse Shoe Bay.

Two women who also worked at the Marina, Marie and Adrienne, became quite friendly and often visited. Adrienne could become very obnoxious when she drank, and one time when Arlene and I were staying there, she came over at night with her problems which she discussed in a loud voice. Larry was always sympathetic and a good listener, but I was unable to get to sleep and eventually got up to tell her there were other people trying to sleep, besides people in the downstairs apartment. Soon after that Adrienne fortunately decided to leave. Larry and Lorraine always got on very well with their co-workers.

CHAPTER II

Lorraine was born to Max Hennigan and me at Bralorne, B.C. on April 23rd, 1939. At that time I had not studied anything about reincarnation, therefore I did not realize then why there was dissension between father and daughter during her growing up years. Lorraine asked about her father in the life reading.

Q: Have Lorraine and her father past life acquaintance?

A: We find them together in the 1400's in Spain. We find the present life father as an almost ten-year older brother. There was not much awareness of each other on the part of the brother and sister, not much closeness. However, as the sister came to a marriageable age, the brother felt quite a sense of responsibility for her. He had a strongly developed sense of the importance of the family, and in that framework it was important that the sister not only marry but make what would be considered a good marriage.

Now the sister, the Lorraine soul in that lifetime, from the soul level had no intention of getting into the feminine experience of marriage. There was no desire evident on the part of the sister to marry. She was not socially inclined. She much preferred her own company. She paid very little attention to the

14

pursuits and activities of young ladies, per-
ferring to spend her time in reading and riding.
This was a matter of much concern to
the brother. He implored the young women he
knew and the sisters of his young men ac-
quaintances to induce her into more feminine
pursuits. He went to great lengths to arrange
meetings for her with the young men he felt
proper for her estate. She was not responsive,
and she never became responsive. The brother
allowed this to be a point of embarassment and
concern to him, so that as the years went a-
long he developed quite a hostility toward her
for her non-responsiveness.
    That element was not worked out in
that lifetime.
    The brother apparently has carried some
of the emotional attitude toward his sister into
this life where they are father and daughter.
There has been a certain inharmony, a certain
prickliness between Lorraine and her Dad.

    I can only remember Max holding Lorraine once
in his arms when I took a picture of them before she
was many weeks old. He never changed a diaper or
fed her during those early months. I feel she needed
more physical contact from the father, and that she
was always in search of the male love that she
needed. When she was forty years old, she had her
first kiss from Max! But much had happened to Lorraine in that intervening time.
    Bralorne is a mining town situated in among
mountains -- at least it was a gold mining town in
1939. Max worked underground and we had saved our
money so he could go commerical fishing. He had
hoped I would be going out with him that spring on
the boat he had been able to purchase, but it was an
impossibility with a young baby. I had felt he may
have held that thwarting of his plans against
Lorraine.

We moved often during Lorraine's formative years and there were often traumatic events. One of these occurred when Lorraine was barely a year old and we were back near Bralorne living at Bradian. We had gone fishing at Fish Lake and that evening I discovered a woodtick at the base of her neck. Fortunately a nurse who was a friend of ours lived close by. Very fortunate, as later that same night it was found that I also had one of these little creatures at the base of my neck. Unfortunate though as this caused me to have a nervous breakdown.

After still another move we were living at Portage, B.C. This place is situated between two large lakes, Anderson and Seton. We lived across Seton Lake where Bridge River and the school were located. Lorraine had to walk along the railroad track several miles to the school, after I had taken her across Seton Lake in a boat. You could go above the one tunnel, but most of the youngsters walked through the tunnel on their way to school. One day I had the intuitive feeling that I should take her in the boat to the other side of the tunnel. When I was back out on the lake, I saw a train going through the tunnel and knew she would have been right in the tunnel at that time. How pleased I was to have followed my intuition.

Still later we were living at Sooke, B.C. about twenty-three miles from Victoria. Temperature there is usually ten degrees lower that it is in Victoria. It is near the sea and there is an excellent harbor. At that time Max had another boat and this was a good location for one. Sooke's only weather problem is that there can be foggy mornings, particulary after several sunny days. For this reason weather seems damper than it is in the city.

When Lorraine was in the higher elementary grades there we lived beside a widow who had five youngsters. One of these, by the name of Donny, (whom his mother called "Dondee") had been very interested in Lorraine. A tragedy occurred, one that

16

was never fully explained. Three boys had gone out in a small boat and only one returned. The other two had drowned. The morning after it had happened, before we even heard of the accident, Lorraine told me she had seen Donny standing in the doorway of our house between the kitchen and front room. It is likely he came there in the spirit form to say goodbye to her.

The first of the family problems with Max began at Sooke. The owner of the place where Donny and his family lived had moved out from the prairies. He was a strange person, possibly because he had been in a war. His main hang-up seemed to be about sex, and since this was at the time when Lorraine had her first boy friend, he seemed to consider it was his business. (Max had gone to Kemano, B.C. for work as a welder at that particular time.)

Two incidents may serve to tell the reader what this person was like. One day he asked me what I thought about using tampax. My glib answer was to immediately reply that would depend on what you were using it for. Another time he got onto astrology and it seems that we were both Leos. Then he mentioned that Leos were careless with their sex. My reply was that that might be true for him but it certainly wasn't for me. So this strange person wrote some kind of a letter to Max about Lorraine and her boy friend, but I never did know quite what. Max immediately returned home and went over to see the neighbor. He never did talk to me first, so that when he finally did I really got mad. The result was a family dispute and ended with Max leaving home. To help weather this bad time, I found myself reading the Sermon on the Mount a lot. It seems that later, after Max returned home, I often quoted from my reading to Lorraine. It was many years later that I found out all my quoting had turned her against religion or a belief in a Supreme Being!

17

That was the second event that had done that to her. The first happened at Bridge River, B.C. when she was much younger and had attended a Sunday School in someone's home. Small copies of the New Testament were given later to those who had had perfect attendance. There were only two children left to be given copies and just one book. The woman gave the copy to her grandson rather than to Lorraine. That influenced her aversion of religion.

CHAPTER III

Two things that had always been stressed in the family were independence and being responsible for one's own actions. At the age of 8, Lorraine had been encouraged to take the bus from Sooke to Victoria and then another bus to Saanich to visit with her grandparents whom she called "Gaw" and "Gawny". We had lived with them prior to the move to Sooke and they thought a lot of her, their first grandchild. At the age of 18, this independence coupled with a search for love, would cause a lot of events to happen.

Lorraine had been quite satisfied with her life at Sooke. She had girl friends she enjoyed being with and was earning money for herself, first from baby sitting, and then by doing waitress work and part-time cooking at the neighborhood cafe. She had attended dancing lessons with many of these friends and she kept her toe shoes ever after. Her sister Louise had also taken lessons and each year the different class members took part in the dancing review. But Lorraine soon towered above many of those she attended class with and in one of the pictures kept from the yearly reviews, she is in the centre because of her growth and maturity.

At Mills Landing High School Lorraine was learning more about nutrition and cooking, as well as how to cut out patterns and to sew. This attribute stood her in good stead the rest of her life. But Max wanted us to move to Kitimat where he would be on steady employment at welding. He was not happy that Lorraine wanted to move with us, especially after

19

the fracas that had occurred at Sooke over the first boy friend. But I was pleased to make the move with both daughters, and even with our two dogs and family cat.

I wanted Lorraine to attend the Kitimat High School, but she was reluctant since she knew no one of her own age. She attended for only a short time, but decided to give that up for a job. Work was easy to obtain then in those early days because the aluminum plants were being built and the place was forging ahead. Because of her cooking ability and experience at Sooke, Lorraine was soon working at the Kitimat Hotel, located near the business section of the town. Since she was blonde, young, attractive, and knew how to dress well, it was not long before her life became complex.

Max made a big issue the time she had a ride home from work with a truck driver. It was his claim that these fellows were only after one thing -- sex. I guess Max never thought about Kitimat Hotel being frequented by taxi drivers!

We did have some family togetherness though. We would go out fishing on the Kitimat River, and when it froze over that first winter, father and daughters all skated on the clear ice. I hadn't known then about Lorraine's involvement. It was only after a friend mentioned to me that she had seen my daughter in a doctor's office, that I found out why she was there. She was pregnant.

Max had once known a fellow who had had great difficulty all of his life because he had been born a bastard. Nothing like that was going to happen in his family, so individually we each met the fellow who was responsible. Craig was a tall good looking fellow, with dark brown curly hair. He and his friend James were both "driving cab" at that time. After some pressure, Craig agreed he would marry Lorraine, but said he would not live with her. We had a small wedding at our Babine Street home with a few friends present and some music afterwards. But Craig left her at home that same night.

Lorraine was never lazy and was always a competent worker. She found other employment away from the hotel and ushered for many months at the Nechako Theater. In August of 1957, George was born, a first grandson for the Hennigans. But Lorraine was not allowed to live at home with this son. She had to be out on her own supporting herself and her child. The ensuing responsibility did much to age her prematurely. Craig did return once to Kitimat, again with his friend James. I believe they were all together for two or three weeks and then the two left for Vancouver, so the time spent with Lorraine and the son was very brief. Perhaps it might have worked if the friend had not been there.

After making an enquiry, I suggested to Lorraine that she fill out an application for work in the Kitimat postal system. Fortunately she was soon hired and was then better able to support herself and son. She obtained a divorce from Craig.

But the inevitable happened. At her work in the Nechako Post Office, she met Peter. He was quite willing to live with her, offered her love, but not marriage. Their son John was born in August of 1959.

Q: Have   Lorraine and   Peter past life acquaintance?

A: They were   in a husband-wife relationship ship, but in reverse roles, in a life in the 1500's A.D. in Central Europe. There was a real love between them which withstood many assaults upon it, for they were both high spirited individuals with minds of their own, and each one had his and her sense of independence. However, they also, each one of them, had a great pride, and in the recognition that in the opinion of their friends the odds were against their making or establishing a

21

continuing marriage, they went forward and established it. Majorly, you see, in that framework of being too proud not to.

Q: She still dreams about him and has a continuing love for him. He is the father of her son, John Carmichael, who was born August 18, 1959 at Kitimat, British Columbia, Canada, approximately 12:15 a.m. so the young man will have his eighteenth birthday this August.

Q: Have Lorraine and her son, John, past life acqaintance?

A: They were in father-daughter relationship, with Lorraine as the father. That was in the lifetime of which I have just spoken, the Middle European lifetime. The natural love expression of the then husband, instead of flowing to the wife flowed to the daughter. This was the most important one in his life and was one of the reasons the marriage was maintained and the home was maintained. He idolized her.
She in turn, responded with a great deal of love and adoration. This was not simply the framework of their relationship when she was a tiny child, but it was the framework of the relationship throughout that lifetime. The daughter in that lifetime even gave up marriage to be with her father in his old age.

The live-in situation with Peter at Kitimat, B.C. did not last long and it became more difficult for her to manage both work and looking after two young ones. Lorraine decided to move to Vancouver, B.C. with George, the older son, and to leave John with a motherly person until she could afford to have him with her as well. She found accommodation in a basement suite and sent for John a few months later.

22

(I remember when she and the boys were in Victoria at Arlene's place and baby John would not leave his mother out of his sight, but kept following her around. He crawled after her everywhere she went.)

By then she needed more than just two rooms and fortunately heard of a new apartment building that was opening. Arlene and I went over to help her move into her new suite. That very first week-end the manager held a get-together for all the new tenants in one of the empty suites. All of us met Ernest at that event.

CHAPTER IV

Ernest and his friend David, had rented one of the suites. Ernest was eight years older than Lorraine. He had come from a broken home, and knew what it was like not to have a family life. Also he loved youngsters and it was not long before he was visiting the mother and her sons often. Ernest offered her marriage and also wanted to adopt the two little boys. Their wedding in Vancouver brought Arlene and me there to help with the arrangements. The couple were married outside of a small church with David and his girl friend in attendance. One of Ernest's sisters held a reception for them at her home.

A daughter, Laverne, was born to them in April of 1963, just three days after Lorraine's own birthday.

Q: Is there past life acquaintance of Lorraine and her daughter Laverne?

A: She too, was a daughter in the 1800's. She has closer ties with the father, and on the soul level has a strong sense of loyalty to him.

Q: The 1800's is the only time she and her mother have been together?

A: Yes.

Q: Will they be together in any future incarnation?

A: That is not patterned. She would have
to build, she would have to initiate that which
would create an interest on the part of the
other soul.

From the suite, the family moved into a nice
home in the Delta area. Both of them were employed
and able to make the necessary house payments.
Lorraine had always loved cats ever since we had
had a black and white one called "Spotty" at Sooke
and Kitimat, so two Siamese cats were added to the
family. Ernest was very handy at improvements. He
made a special small opening in the back door so the
two cats could go in and out at will. He also worked
at the completion of unfinished basement rooms. Max
and I came down from Terrace, B.C. to spend that
first Christmas with them and Arlene came over from
Victoria. We really appreciated the way Ernest had
become a real father to all three of the young ones.
      Lorraine's postal experience enabled her to
find work in a nearby area and she suddenly became
the first female person in charge of mail carriers in
Canada. An article about this feat appeared in the
Toronto Star newspaper after she was interviewed.
      The boys were attending school at this time.
Lorraine had always kept them nicely dressed and at
one time made matching outfits for the two boys,
herself, and her sister, Louise. The seven and a half
years between the sisters did not matter now both
had become adults, and they became good friends.
      Somehow Lorraine seemed to feel a lack of
affection from her parents and we were told that
was what prompted a sudden decision for a family
move to be made to Australia. The cats were given
away to good homes, the essentials were crated and
sent on their way. Max and I made a special weekend

25

flight to say farewell to them all. At that time we had moved to Nass Camp where I was the intermediate teacher and then principal of Nass River Elementary. Mail to the Camp took longer than it did to Terrace because of the 70 mile drive on logging roads.

Only about two weeks after we had said goodbye, we received a post card from Australia which told us not to be surprised if the family would be arriving back. Louise could not believe the news. The card arrived one day and the family the next. Louise believed it when she spoke to her sister on the phone.

It seems the crated family goods arrived one day in Australia and were sent back to Canada on the next.

It turned out that Australia was like Canada had been thirty years previous and Ernest had been reminded of his past, when his parents had split up and he had been sent to live in different foster homes, until an older sister looked after him.

Lorraine resented the low status women had in Australia. A woman had no say at all and any questions of importance were directed to the man in the family. Added to that, it was not easy to locate any work and the promise of warm water to swim in hadn't mentioned the presence of sharks.

Q: Have Lorraine and her father other past life acquaintance besides that 1400's Spanish one?

A: Yes. They had a very good relationship as brother and sister in a lifetime in which the Eleanor Loraine soul was the brother and the father soul was the sister. This was a life in the 1200's A.D. It was a lifetime in Italy. The sister was about a year and a half older than the brother. This had a certain advantage, in

26

that as a very imaginative child she thought up many games for them to play and was the leader in their pursuits together in early childhood.

As they grew older they each, as it were, fell into their own pattern of doing according to their own role in life, and the circumstances were such that their lives did not impinge upon one another very frequently. But they had a basic goodwill between them and they did have some pleasant childhood memories which they shared.

Q: Could we know what further happened to that 1200's personality of the Lorraine soul. What was the man's work and his own life?

A: At a rather early age he was apprenticed -- that is not quite the right word -- he became the personal server to a gentleman of the court, and proving himself intelligent, proving himself obedient, most of all proving himself capable of holding his tongue, gradually advanced himself, becoming in time a trusted and loyal message bearer between the then court of Italy and other established courts on the Continent.

We guess today you might speak of him as a foreign diplomat, although he did not play a part in establishing decisions. He simply carried messages.

Now there was quite an element of intrigue among the ruling families at that time, and to correctly and safely carry a given message and deliver it at the time it was to be delivered and in the place and to the person, was no mean accomplishment. He was excellent in that activity, and won the respect and the notice of the court with resultant honors being heaped upon him.

Q: What do you suggest to Lorraine about
the relationship with her father? He is still
alive. Would it be good for her to become more
gracious with him or something?

A: Yes. We think she could make overtures
of kindly solicitation, of interest in his activities and so forth.

Lorraine became the first woman to be hired
as a cook at Nass Camp. I think this is also where
she learned to use four letter words easily. She did,
after all, get on very well with men, and she wasn't
the type who would not say "damn." Ernest, in the
meantime, found work to do that he was used to .
Max Hennigan had been a conservationist for
many years. He had been the one who brought to
light the fact that the Aluminum Company of Canada
had been allowing raw sewage to go into the Kitimat
River. Max had also been active in union work and
his daughter became a member at the Camp.
Besides baking fresh bread and many goodies,
and organizing all the meals and lunches, Lorraine
spent some of her spare hours at home, sewing. At
that job she did often lose patience, but one young
woman had a very special wedding gown made for her
by Lorraine.
Like her father, Lorraine was a conservationist
and particulary fond of animals. One day she was
aghast when a fellow at the camp shot another
person's dog in the mouth and the dog ran home to
die. Later on when it was suggested this same fellow
should become the Camp Manager, she took it upon
herself to write to the Vancouver office as to why
he would not be a good person for that job.
It was probably held against her, just as things
were held against Max whenever he complained about
debris being put into the rivers during the company's
logging. It was like father — like daughter in regard

28

to what is termed blacklisting.

A new company took over the cookhouse and Lorraine was told she would no longer be working there. She went on strike and there was one mad morning during which Ernest drove her to the gate at Terrace and nobody came up to work that day! However, she lost out even though her claim was taken up by the union grievance committee.

It wasn't too many months later that Lorraine and Ernest decided to move their trailer to a warmer clime. Having camped before in the Penticton area, they decided to move their trailer down that way. Max and I also moved from Nass Camp that same year but our destination was Masset, where Louise and family were located.

Lorraine was always conscious of appearance — she didn't want to look old. There were several operations she had that were probably for that purpose. One operation she had was to make her breasts smaller — according to her these were too heavy a weight to carry around. I remember she gave me the brassieres she discarded! My policy is to grow older gracefully which is something to do with inner quality that keeps people looking younger than their years. I think that operation was really for a more youthful bust line! Earlier she had had her varicose veins stripped. Another time it was an operation near the eyes. The hysterectomy probably was a needed one, but in my opinion it is not a good idea to interfere with the body one has inherited in this life. To my mind one could be asking for future trouble.

CHAPTER V

Now we must return to Horse Shoe Bay where Lorraine and Larry were working at the Marina and were friendly with Marie and Adrienne. Things did not always go well between Lorraine and Larry. Perhaps it was because he really was lazy, or that she objected to him drinking wine when she didn't. Whatever happened, there was a definite rift.

The relationship floundered in 1981 and they decided to go their separate ways. Lorraine wanted more than ever to return to the sunshine of Maui. Ernest still hoped for a reconciliation. It was arranged that Arlene and I would spend a month at a condominium at Maalaea with Laverne, her mother and her father, Ernest. It was a different Christmas. We bought what Lorraine termed an "old clunker," and so managed to get to all of the special places, particulary to Onealoa Beach, better known as Makena. We were like any visitors who ever go to this beach -- it somehow becomes the favorite beach to go to.

Since the sun goes down very early, we spent our evenings playing many different games, even Monopoly. When you leave a temperate climate where the sun stays in sight longer, it becomes a little difficult changing the hours for sleeping and waking.

The reconciliation Ernest had wished for did not take place. Lorraine decided she would stay on at Maui and looked in the daily paper for opportunity. She read of the need for a companion who would cook and stay with an elderly lady. As it happened the lady lived only a few doors away, and after an interview, Lorraine accepted the position. She had her own little place to stay and in addition to the cooking she only needed to do the shopping and to take the small dog for a daily walk. Each morning she enjoyed a long walk along the beach as the main house was right on the waterfront.

It seems that wasn't enough to keep her happy; she felt much alone and bereft. One day she happened to feel a lump on one breast under her bathing suit. It grew quickly. She consulted a doctor who advised her to take the next plane back to Canada. In her distraught condition, she phoned Larry telling him of her plight. He agreed to meet her at the Vancouver airport.

Their friend Adrienne quite liked Larry and had even considered sharing the apartment expenses with him after Lorraine left.

It was while she was waiting for the plane to take her to Vancouver that Lorraine had a strange experience. Apparently she was out of her body and met Larry in the astral, and to her he confessed to having shared a bottle of wine with Adrienne and going to bed with her.

Immediately after Lorraine met Larry at the airport, she told Larry of this strange experience. His face went chalk white. Somehow he had shared the same experience with her in the astral.

The doctor in Vancouver termed the lump a malignant one, and Lorraine agreed to a mastectomy. Owing to the prompt attention, the surgeon told them the cancer had been contained, and no further treatment would be needed. While in the hospital, shortly after the operation, Ernest came to visit her. Soon Larry and Arlene came in the door. Although it was a tense moment, the two shook hands in a greeting across the bed where Lorraine lay. Larry and Lorraine renewed their relationship.

An implant the following year improved the breast appearance and helped to restore Lorraine's self-approval. At all times she kept herself attrac-

31

tively dressed. Her cooking and sewing competency were attributes from which we all profited.

Lorraine became the chief cook at Kiwanis Manor while Larry was employed as a waiter and bartender in a large hotel in West Vancouver. They had rented an apartment in North Vancouver and three of them shared the expenses as Larry had persuaded Lorraine to allow her daughter Laverne to move in with them.

At that time Lorraine was aware that she had hypoglycemia symptoms and she usually watched her food intake carefully. But one night they drove up to Whistler to visit with a cousin of Larry's and her husband. She with her hearty appetite could not resist indulging in chocolate fondue. On the drive home, Lorraine commented that she hoped there would be no ill effects as chocolate was on the "no no" list of foods.

It was the following morning at her work as the chef of Kiwanis Manor that she suddenly collapsed. A nurse came down from the upper floor with oxygen and an ambulance was called. Lorraine was in the hospital as soon as possible. Stangely enough, she was unable to speak or write but could visualize the words she should be saying. No one knew she should not be given sugar and she was given intravenous feeding. Early that same evening a neurologist came to see her and she found it very difficult to trace over a few letters. However, she was discharged that same evening and Larry took her home. There she took what appeared to be an epileptic fit -- she could not speak, but kept gesticulating to her mouth. She was taken a glass of water, then a bucket and finally some yogurt. After she had eaten the yogurt she was again able to speak.

Residents at Kiwanis Manor seem to have no difficulty whenever tests are prescribed. But when Lorraine's doctor wanted her to have a CAT scan, he was unable to arrange an appointment for her.

Lorraine kept working, and although she could not always put in a full day's shift, she did manage to be in full charge of the annual Hawaiian night dinner. The array of food would delight a gourmet, and I was even allowed to take a picture of her that night when she was wearing her high white hat.

CHAPTER VI

It wasn't until Lorraine began to bump into things that her doctor was able to have the scan taken. By then there had been days when she could only be at work for an hour or two. The day she drove herself to her doctor's office to find out the result of the scan was the last time she drove herself home. She'd been told she had a malignant inoperable tumor of the brain.

My sister and I had gone back over to Victoria by then and Larry relayed the news to us by phoning a cousin first. It was our turn for devastation. Immediately we went over on the ferry to be with them. Lorraine felt she only had five weeks left and it was her wish to spend those last weeks on Maui, her favorite island in Hawaii.

Lorraine and Larry arranged an appointment with the cancer specialist in order to see the scan themselves. It was clearly visible where the two small tumors had merged into one, which was what had probably happened when she collapsed at the manor.

The cancer specialist was asked by Lorraine how long he felt she had to live -- "Christmas? the Fall?, the Summer?" He told her in his opinion she had three weeks left at the most. He prescribed 4 decatron tablets daily. In response to her enquiry about their effect, she was told that in a week or ten days she would lose all her muscle control and become a "blob." He also suggested putting her into the hospital so a needle could be inserted and the tumor checked on that way, but she refused that suggestion.

Decatron is said to remove the fluid from around a tumor in order to lessen pain. It was Lorrain's decision to curtail the amount she would take and instead of the four daily, she would only take one quarter of a tablet in the evening before going to sleep.

At the time of this happening Larry and Lorraine had moved into a comfortable basement suite. Laverne had moved in with a former friend at that time; expenses needed to be cut. They had put an ad into the paper mentioning an "old and boring couple" in need of a basement suite. Lynn had just happened to read that particular paper and after the couple had seen the suite, they rented it from Lynn immediately. Lynn lived in the upstairs suite with her teenage daughter. Lynn and Lorraine got on very well together and had become good friends. It was Lynn who came into the new wardrobe Lorraine had fashioned for herself for the fall -- everything fitted Lynn well and even their shoe size was the same!

The night Lynn was trying on the clothes was the night Ernest called in after he had received a phone call about her health. He had been very upset. He did say he thought he could get some Taheebo tea for her, but he couldn't cope with her clothes being given away. Lorraine had stated "Nobody will want my clothes after I'm dead," and immediately Lynn had been invited down to model them.

We were back over with them in North Vancouver that evening and the following one when Larry suddenly asked Lorraine if she would like to be married. At first she could not believe her ears, but we assured her that we had heard his question also. This was something she had wanted for a long while and her response was that she would will herself so that they would be married.

Lorraine was the one who searched the newspapers and found a condo available for rent at Kamaole III Beach. We had already made arrange-

35

ments to leave as soon as possible for Maui and Lorraine's "Auntie," my sister, had already cashed in retired saving money to cover expenses. It was decided we could make good use of the 1966 Buick in Maui, and it could be left later in the double garage of the house Arlene and I were buying there. Lorraine found out just when the Matson line would have a boat leaving for the island. On the Thursday morning Arlene and I drove the car to Seattle and returned to Vancouver by bus as soon as we could. It was there in time to sail that same afternoon on the boat. The car would be handy since Larry's brother was going to be best man at the wedding, and Lorraine's daughter, Laverne, was going to be her bridesmaid. Our tickets were for the Saturday morning.

We had brought with us to Vancouver a supply of herbs and Taheebo tea, everything a relative of Arlene's could provide to combat a tumor, from her Nature's Sunshine supply of herbs. All of the instructions were relayed to Laverne, who had only just recently decided she would like to become a nurse, and it was she who kept all the herbs ready for her mother. We were well stocked with these special supplies as Ernest also brought over some of the tea.

That same Thursday we returned to Victoria to prepare for the stay on Maui. We had put on the answering machine while we were away briefly and returned to a message from Lorraine.

"Larry and I are going out for dinner. The doctor was very optimistic and we will phone you again later."

From the later communication we found out Lorraine would be going on the Friday to the Holistic Centre in West Vancouver. That day before we were to leave there were many visitors coming to wish them both well — John and his girl friend picked out a wedding gift for them. Another close girl friend brought them a single white candle in a holder.

That day Lorraine had three sessions at the

Holistic Centre -- "Believability -- keep the mind clear." She was able to put herself in a trance to get away from the pain and we were all happy with the change in her attitude.

Her son George flew out with his son, Kyle, from Edmonton. Max had sent down money by registered mail, as well as a letter. Laverne and her boy friend stayed most of the evening and many of Larry's relatives were among those visiting. Laverne made Tabeebo tea to be taken on the plane and had all the herbs arranged for a day's intake. The three visits need a separate chapter.

CHAPTER VII

FIRST VISIT

The Holistic Centre Lorraine went to was managed by a father and son by the name of Judd. First Lorraine was shown how to channel her energy to combat the tumor. I have since read scientific data in regard to tumors that states, "The brain gives forth a morphinelike chemical responsible for the lessening of pain. This substance is 200 times as powerful as morphine. It is called dynorphin, one of a family of exciting brain chemicals called endorphins. These chemicals are a major part of the body's defenses. Evidence suggests hypnosis releases endorphin from the brain during tumors."

At the Holistic Centre Lorraine was found to be an ideal subject for hypnosis. For many years, ever since the double life reading had been done she had wanted to be regressed to former lives. Her chief interest had been Maui, but conductor Jerry Judd on that first visit took her back to her first incarnation.

In that first lifetime, Lorraine described herself as being a man named Nareeka. He and his wife and son lived in a small hut. All the tribe members lived in huts close to a river and there was lots of tall grass nearby. A tall animal was described, one which fitted the description of a giraffe. Members of the tribe chiefly existed on eating a small animal much like a rabbit. The women stayed at home while the men hunted for food. Although they lived close to a river, no fishing was done. No date was given, but it appeared to be in the distant past.

SECOND VISIT

On each visit the ability to channel the energy to combat the tumor was reinforced by the conductor. On the second visit, Lorraine was regressed to a previous life on Maui. She was a woman named Taheeto, born in the year 1800. Excerpts from that lifetime were relived -- when she first met Lareeto (Larry) near the black rocks on Big Beach (also known as Oneola or Makena Beach, the very spot Larry and Lorraine had been drawn to during their few months holiday on Maui prior to working at the Marina in North Vancouver near Horse Shoe Bay). Lareeto was ten years younger than she was, and she left her husband and three youngsters to live with him. Another excerpt was when both stood at Makena Landing close to where the Keawala'i Church is today, and watched boats sailing out in the harbour. (During the Maui holiday they had often walked past this particular place.) In the final excerpt, she was 43 years old and was living alone in a sparsely furnished shack which was built on pilings. (There are houses similary raised there today.) At that particular happening she had a bowl of rice which she ate with her hands. Then she curled up on a small mat in the fetal position and died. She was so alone and bereft that she sobbed and cried uncontrollably. Immediately the conductor brought her back to this life. It was following that session that she said she never wanted to live on Maui again.

THIRD VISIT

This time conductor Jerry took Lorraine a little further along in time. The year was 1632, and she described herself as being senile. The location was Finland where the narrow streets and tall buildings were described. Noreen Fredrica was twenty-three years of age and a spinster. In her words she had on a "grey gown, big boots, and a stupid hat."

Before leaving the Holistic Centre after the third visit, both Michael and Jerry asked that she come to see them after the trip to Maui. A tape was given to her that could be played whenever she felt the need -- reinforcement of the channelling of the energy.

The night before we left Larry talked to Lorraine's sister, Louise, who lived on the Queen Charlotte Islands with her family. Louise had not been able to understand her sister's need and pull to this island of Maui. Larry, in his personable way, was able to tell the sister about the day's full happenings and why we all agreed on this need to follow Lorraine's wishes.

Saturday morning we left for the destination of Maui, having taken leave of friends and relatives, and leaving behind us the purchased tickets for "Evita," which was coming to the Queen Elizabeth Theatre in August. This was a play Lorraine wanted to see and one of her favorite songs was, "Don't Cry For Me, Argentina."

CHAPTER VIII

On May 25th, 1985, we arrived at the condo we had rented from people in Vancouver (Lorraine had seen the advertisement and done the phoning!) We were on the ground floor right across from Kamaole Beach III right beside the swimming pool. Four of us had flown over together -- Lorraine, Laverne, Arlene and I. Larry arrived the next day. Arlene phoned the United Church minister and made an appointment for Lorraine and Larry to see him at 4 p.m.. The wedding was to take place at 4 p.m. on June 4th in the Keawala'i Church.

At the condo we found a portable sewing machine in the kitchen closet. Later we found the owners had not even known it was there. Immediately Lorraine and Laverne thought perhaps they would make dresses for the wedding. So besides utilizing the pool and the salt water, we made a trip into Kahului for dress material. That very night the cutting and measuring began. In a phone call with the family at the Charlottes, we heard one of Louise's daughters had seen Max ("grandpa"). She had been in sports competition at Terrace, but he hadn't stayed long to visit as he was too upset about Lorraine.

The day after the material had been bought, Lorraine had her dress completely pinned together, and a train as well. One more day and the wedding dress was finished complete with an added ruffle at the bottom of the dress. Then Laverne got busy on her sewing. Then even Arlene and I made ourselves dresses, simple ones with lace overblouses.

Larry had his brother James there to be his best man. Another brother who was unable to come over, paid for the couple to spend two nights in a honeymoon suite at the Intercontinental Hotel. The few friends Larry and Lorraine had made when they were there in 1976, were invited to the wedding.

Larry covered the buttons for the wedding dress. While they were together she also taught him how to sew and two of the first things he made were small round beds with sides on them for their two cats. Ming, who was to have been Larry's cat, seemed to be the favorite. When we spoke to Lynn at North Vancouver one night, Ming had been missing for three days and Lorraine shed tears over this, her first ones for sometime. Fortunately he later returned -- he no doubt missed his family.

The car reached Maui the day before the wedding. On that same day a tape arrived in the mail from the Judds, one she could listen to at anytime. Things had not gone well for Lorraine that day so both arrivals were timely. No doubt her lack of zest and energy was to be expected after the effort she had been making. The news she hadn't liked was that the pool was going to be closed for two weeks -- it was a hardship for her to cross the road and make the trek to the salt water. That was the day she said how sorry she was for our sake.

It was a lovely wedding on June 4th -- a typical Hawaiian one: both were barefoot and wore the maile leis. Larry was in white save for a rose colored sash. Lorraine had a head lei. Both looked extremely happy. The minister had invited someone to play the guitar and sing -- his wife was a hula dancer. The man, Garry, had been cured of both a brain tumor and leukemia. These two joined the other few friends who had been invited to a small reception at the condo. The double wedding rings had been engraved with their 1800 names -- Lareeto and Taheeto.

Larry had bought his bride-to-be an elegant negligee in a purple shade. Larry took pictures of her in the bridal suite, and we can see in the negligee picture how tired Lorraine looks after all the excitement, but none of this shows in the wedding photos. At the reception Garry had told us how he had been cured seven weeks previously by a minister who did healing and Larry had made an appointment there for himself and his wife. Lorraine was unfortunately unable to accept the needed belief in God, and so there was to be no cure for her there, no "healing," even though on a second visit they both saw the minister who had done the healing.

We were still making the Taheebo tea and Laverne continued to count out the special herbs for each day. The tape she had been sent to play began to become monotonous, and when we had read of a lecture to be given by hynotherapist Dr. Irvine Katz, Arlene and I and the newlyweds decided to attend. Larry made a special arrangement for the two of them to have a private appointment, and at this consultation "Irv" K. made her another tape. He felt her life would make a great movie, which inspired me to immediately write a story entitled "The Pull of Maui," which ended with the double ring ceremony and the names on their rings. Loraine enjoyed reading it very much.

There was a phone call from Louise again on the sixth of June. She mentioned having seen her sister in the hall and thought Lorraine had died. One of the sisters could have been astral traveling!

Lorraine was not sleeping well and one day could hardly walk at all. Someone stayed with her all the time. From a phone call to Dr. Irvine K. we were told emotions cause fear which in turn causes pain. He would make another tape for them on calming the fear. That helped. But Lorraine developed a sore throat so went to see a doctor. Once again she was told to take the next plane home to Vancouver. Fortunately there were two seats left on the plane and they were able to arrange to leave that same day.

When we phoned Vancouver, Larry and Lorraine were out in the sun and Larry's cat, Ming
would not leave them alone. Lorraine's cat, Polaris
was happy to see them as well, but was not as af-
fectionate as Ming -- different personalities.
There appears to be a spiritual link between us
and our pets. Perhaps there is a dimension somewhere, unknown to us, where we will meet with these
companions as well.

In her life reading Franklin Loehr stated:
Reincarnation is one of the basic elements of the spirit. In other words, one of the
basic elements of the non-physical portion of
us is the spirit which will have an incarnation
here, and then at the death of that body, without an incarnate expression for a while and
then come back with another incarnation somewhere else. So she has an opening in the opening to reincarnation. She has an opening to, as
it were, interest in the spirit.

Lorraine was quoted as saying: "I was an agnostic
bordering on atheism for many years, until I discovered reincarnation."

Dr. Loehr goes on to explain:
Reincarnation does deal with the soul...
The root meaning of the word spiritual is
simply non-material... Religion deals in this
area...It is also the area of woman...An ancient
symbol of masculine and feminine was the
cross. The crossbar represented the masculine
-- told to go out and take dominion over the
earth...The feminine represented the vertical
line, the upsweep to values and to contact
with other realms, other realities beyond the
surface of the earth.

Certainly reincarnation is one of the basic elements of the spirit. In other words, one of the basic elements of the non-physical portion of us is the spirit which will have an incarnation here, and then at the death of that body, continue without an incarnate expression for a while, and then came back with another incarnation somewhere else. So Lorraine has an opening to interest in the spirit in her opening to reincarnation.

The Sunday before Arlene and I were able to make our return flight to Vancouver, we attended the little church where Lorraine and Larry had been married. Prayers were said for her that day at Keawalai'i. People in many other churches on Maui, in Victoria, and in Vancouver also had her on their prayer lists.

Following the advice received in Maui at the medical centre, Lorraine expressed the wish to be back in Vancouver with her friends, enjoying her own bed. She also went again with Larry to the Holistic Centre to be able to work on her own energy, as well as to be regressed. At that time, Lorraine made two tapes of previous lives, one when she was in the male role and the other when she was in the female role.

First, Lorraine describes herself as being a male person named Abdullah, dressed in a galabea. He then went on to describe himself as being skinny, of an average height, but on the short side, with a moustache. At the age of thirty-three he spoke of himself as whistling while walking past cream walls.

"The sky is blue, the boats are beautiful and their sails are bright. The town is by the sea and the name is Phoenicia. The buildings are

45

square-shaped in a creamy off-white shade with a small dome."

"Yes, I'm married and have one child."

A little further along in that lifetime, Abdullah was flaying his arms and whistling. Again he describes the galabea he is wearing and the turban. There is kind of a fancy embroidery on the garment and he is wearing leather sandals.

"My feet are really dark." "I seem to be happy. I'm very very happy -- wife's just had another baby. I'm thirty-four and this is my second child. We're not too well off but I seem to be happy. In fact, I'm very very happy."

Q: "Do you recognize anyone?"

"My second child, who is male. He is my favorite child -- Cashubal-blonde and handsome. His hair is a little frilly on the top. My wife's name is Livia."

In response to more questioning, Abdullah said he went out on the boats for his living. It took some thought for him to know just what he did, but he was a navigator at the front of the boat.

"And I love it -- beautiful blue sparkling water."

The merchant ship he worked on delivered things to Fanetica, which really wasn't too far away. Abdullah was happy. In response to a question about the cargo:

"I don't think I care."

Then he did mention tea and vases, also that the rest of the men were inlanders.

"Buildings are off-white and there are lots of birds. It's a pretty place."

Instructions were given to go ahead in time, to see if anyone could be recognized.

Q: "Who's with you?"

"It's George and he's twenty and he still had blonde hair which is really unusual. It's a little dark and curly. He's tall and skinny, the same as now. He doesn't smile much — is wearing a diaper style loin cloth, but we're in the house.

I have an older child, a female. I don't bother much about her. Her name is Albion and she's a dancer — like the Far East, wearing jewels — almost like a belly-type of dancing. She and her mother spend a lot of time together."

Many oohs and ahs are heard coming from Abdullah in a very frightened and concerned way.

"The streets are busy. We're being invaded somehow. There's cannon fire. Ooh, Ooh, Ooh! Maybe I'm dead, I don't know. The noises have stopped. Maybe it was a false alarm after all. People are running around. I feel confident now. Everything will be all right. The family's all in my house."

Conductor: "What was that all about?"

"I don't seem to know."

47

Conductor: "You'll be somewhat detached, looking at it from a distance."

"There are people on horses coming down and attacking. It wasn't as important as we thought, it wasn't too bad. It's a scattered incident."

Conductor: "What people?"

"They're almost like bandits — people who live out in the desert. It's an isolated incident as it were. I can't think of their name. My people must have beaten them back. It wasn't cannon fire — basically some kind of muskets of an antique type, long and thin."

Conductor: "What year is it Abdullah?"

"It's five something."

Conductor: "I'll count three, snap my fingers and you'll give me the year."

"Oh, it's 562 A.D."

Conductor: "You'll reexperience the attack, but you'll be completely calm and detached."

"I'm coming down the street going home when there are noises and panic starts. Everyone is panicking. I know I have to get home. It's mostly gunfire, but there some larger noises like explosions. People are rushing around. But I'm fine now, I'm fine.

Conductor: "How old are you now Abdullah?"

"Oh, I'm dying. I'm forty something, I'm not sure. Oh, I'm fifty, that's old, but I still look pretty good."

Q: "What's wrong with you?"

"I'm just ill. I haven't been ill for very long though, just a short while. My wife is with me. I'm lying down, but I'm not sad. I'm closer to my daughter now as well.

"I'm moving."

Q: "How do you feel?"

"I'm looking down, it's not too sad. It's O.K. It's not too bad. It's O.K. I'm calm, very calm and peaceful. It's not too bad at all."

CHAPTER IX

There was a question about George in Lorraine's Life Reading.

Q: "Have Lorraine and her son, George, pastlife experience?

A: "George was a son of that 1800's life. On the soul level he does not carry much expectation of receiving from his mother. She provided the opportunity for him to come into this earthlife and he wanted in and that is all right. But he really does not have much of a sense, an inner sense, or a feeling of the mother-son relationship, not much more than she has."

Q: "Any suggestion to Lorraine in regard to her son, George?"

A: "Just the one suggestion that we make in all her family relationships, that if she chooses to she can initiate a growing meaningful relationship."

The life in Phoenicia where she recognized George in the person of Cashubal, was not mentioned. However the lives we are told about are those which have a direct bearing on the current one, especially if there is some wrong we need to make aright.

Lorraine called George her "Number one son" and John her "Number two son." Laverne was "Short One."

When Abdullah was describing his galabea and turban, and looked at his leather sandals, it is quite obvious that his skin was a very dark color. Perhaps that was partly why Lorraine was always out in the sun wanting to be a dark tan. She had been happy in Phoenicia.

The second tape concerns the life with Max when they were sister and brother. This was the life in Spain in the 1400's which was mentioned earlier, from her life reading. The recorded version follows:

"I'm female. My hair is parted in the middle. I'm wearing an off-shoulder dress. It's not a bright dress. It's very nice. I'm even normal weight — I'm not fat again. It's a typical life. I'm an old maid, but I enjoy it. I'm thirty. My name is Erin.

My house is really nice. It's one of those big type ones. I seem to be happy -- that's strange because that's a female life. I don't have a boy friend even — just my dogs and horses. I seem to have some servants, but I like to an- swer the door myself. We're quite well off."

Instructions were given to move back to an earlier incident at the count of three.

"I'm ten. We're sitting on the ground having a picnic. Yes. I don't think I ever moved. My parent's name is Georgia. I don't know my father. He's kind of stern. My grandfather from this life seems to be my father and we were never close in this life, not at all. We're not close. There's my brother, who is my father now -- he's younger than me. I'm ten and he's six."

Q: Are you happy?

"Yes, I'm happy."

Q: Do you have a good relationship with your mother?

"Yes, very good, but nobody is around after awhile. I seem to have the place to myself.

Conductor: We'll move ahead to find a focal point.

"I'm in the library again browsing through my books, not so much reading them. I speak Spanish."

Conductor: Say something in your language.

"I can't quite get it out." (She laughs.) There was the sound of two very quickly spoken Spanish sentences, then the comment, "I can't quite get my tongue around the words. Easy, easy, little things I know even now," and she quickly rattled off several.

Conductor: I'll count three and you'll go ahead.

"I'm riding my horse, I'm riding side-saddle, very lady-like fashion (you could hear the surprise in her voice inflection.) That's surprising — I have a dress on yet. It's a beautiful horse, shining, shining. It's a magnificent animal. I have a crop but I don't use it. I'm going down a long path, not a trail — it's a long wide open space away from the house. It's just beautiful, just magnificent. The sun is shining, shining (You hear pleasure in all these statements). I do love to ride my horse."

"There's a party in our house (this sounded to be unusual), quite a few people -- a nice friendly party, everyone's dressed up. It's a big room and more people are coming. I have some nice friends. We're really well-to-do and never have to work. I have no boy friends. The only antagonism is my brother, but I think he's given up and doesn't bother me now. I'm enjoying myself.

"I seem to be forty. I'm definitely an old maid, but still enjoying myself. I have the large house, my library, horses and friends. I have servants -- someone who cooks too. I like to open the door myself. It's a nice peaceful life. I'm completely happy, completely relaxed."

Before bringing Lorraine back to the present, she was told she would notice how good she felt and that she would be perfectly relaxed. M. Judd then asked her why she had chosen those two lives and she told him,

"Because they were happy lives, and I've had so few of these."

There is a slight discrepancy as to which member of the family was the older in the Spanish life, but the error could have been made in the life reading transcript. Judging by her own words I feel the sister was ten years older than her brother.

CHAPTER X

Shortly before Laverne, Arlene "Auntie" and I left Maui we heard from Lorraine who had been sitting out in the sun all day. Temperature had been 89. She had had her third good day and requested that we get her a large-size dress since she had eaten so much. From someone else in Vancouver, we heard she believed her tumor had gone. It was when we arrived back with the large dress and a pink negligee for her as well, that we heard about the two tapes having been made.

Ernest had phoned to Lorraine after he had had word from us, which explained why the phone had been busy the night before we flew back. We heard that same night from a cousin who was sending over Lorraine's Egyptian dress and when he'd mentioned a friend would be bringing over more herbs Lorraine told him it would be cheaper for her to die as the herbs would cost her between two and three hundred dollars a month.

Early in 1985 Lorraine had made a trip to Egypt on her own and taken a lot of pictures. When Larry showed us these slides one night, Lorraine kept up a commentary for us and then went to bed.

Arlene and I returned to Victoria. I made a few copies of "The Pull of Maui" that I had written on Maui and which the daughter quite enjoyed. That one ended with the double ring ceremony at Keawala'i Church.

It was possibly ten days later that we heard Lorraine wasn't well, she had had little sleep and was having difficulty walking, so Arlene went over and at their request stayed with them. One night Laverne took a walker over for her mother since once when she was alone Lorraine had been unable to walk. For this reason when Arlene came back to Victoria I went over to Vancouver -- our ferries crossed en route. For the first time Lorraine took a whole decatron as she had had such a bad day. I'd used the foot bath and rubbed her legs and neck with tei-fu. It was the next day that she received a phone call about a healer from the Philippines, and the caller promised her some free tapes on cancer, which Lynn from upstairs said she would pick up. At about this time Max was making arrangements to come down with Louise to see Lorraine -- he just didn't want me to be there!

In a visit made by Lorraine and Larry to M. Judd's, the latter felt the family needed to show more physical love to Lorraine, and probably to others in the family as well. Son George had phoned from Edmonton that he would be coming out early in August. Arrangements were being made whereby Lorraine and her Auntie Arlene would be making an appointment to see the psychic surgeon. Larry's sister-in-law, Maybelle would also go with them.

I worked on a hug and a kiss to my daughter at least once a day and when we relayed the love suggestion to her son John, he did likewise. This resulted in a few tears from Lorraine, but later she was laughing instead.

The day before the three left was not a good one -- several weeping and sobbing spells. In one of these she wanted us to promise that we would look after "short one."

I think the trip itself was a very wearing one for Lorraine, but a phone call was made to us on the evening of the first appointment. From the bed (and Lorraine always was one to be there early), she mentioned her experience. She could feel the surgeon's finger nails going into her head and thought the ordeal would hurt, but it did not. Two patients went in at one time so that each witnessed the operation on the other. Lorraine had witnessed the surgeon remove a growth from one person's eye. Another time she saw him put his hands on a woman's stomach; immediately the stomach opened up and he lifted out a growth, which appeared to be solid until it was held over a basin by his assistant. The woman who assisted then wiped up the blood. After the growth was removed in that way, Lorraine saw the stomach go back together.

According to Arlene, after the arrival of all the patients, everyone was assembled in a large room where the psychic surgeon spoke to them. He explained that his hands were the "hands of God." His spirit guides would only allow him to remove part of a tumor at a time. His hands were magnetic and knew just where to go. In regard to brain tumors, he said he could remove and cure 85% of those he operated on, but that if he could do 100% he would be God.

At Lorraine's first visit, he called her "Big Momma" and joked with her. He was sure she would be all right.

Arlene went with Lorraine to the next appointment on the following morning, and has said she will never forget the look on the surgeon's face. He apparently knew then that she was not going to get better. That same session, my sister watched him remove a growth from Lorraine's groin, and another long piece that looked like fish roe, from low down on her neck. Both of these areas had appeared swollen to us for several weeks, but had never seemed to cause Lorraine any discomfort.

Prior to any patient entering the operating room, he or she was given energy by means of holding hands and by prayers. It seems this psychic type of healing is considered just ordinary procedure in the Philippines. We seem to be behind the times in the North American continent; unfortunately sometimes greed and ignorance go together. It was a long time in British Columbia before chiropractors were

56

allowed to come under health coverage. Public opinion has helped to bring about many improvements.

At the healing centre. there had been one fellow who commented he didn't really know why he was there and who sounded quite skeptical. A day later they met again and he pulled up his shirt to show them the scar he had -- no doubt that had occurred because of his having been somewhat dubious about the healing, since this is the only case we have heard of where that had resulted. However, we know there are lots of scars or scar tissue to be seen following many medical operations, and they are not there on the day following the operation.

One day people were asked if two appointments could be given up because someone needed these who would be arriving, but who had not made the previous arrangements. Lorraine believed the woman was a well-known former movie actress whom she did not recognize; the man driving the car only commented that he did not know why he was there, so all of the arrangements seemed to have been kept very quiet.

It was a very long and tiring return trip and Lorraine must also have been quite disappointed. She told me one night she wished it had worked out, as she would have liked me to have written about it, but I am writing about it anyway.

One Sunday Mark Spielman held a special seminar which Lorraine and Arlene attended. Lorraine volunteered to be regressed and at that time could only think of the life on Maui in the 1800's. She relived the disposition of the body there following her death and looking down, saw her body thrown off a cliff for a sea burial.

It seems at that seminar when under hypnosis and told to move certain fingers up for "yes" or "no," Lorraine when asked if she wanted to get better, twice put up the "no" finger, and only at the last managed the one finger for a "yes." Perhaps that all day session, coupled with tiredness after the long trip, had overtaxed her strength.

It was about this time that the play "Evita" was to be performed on stage at the Queen Elizabeth Theatre, but Lorraine was not going to be able to go, so suggested her ticket be used by her good friend Ella, instead. That night Lynn's daughter offered to stay home with Lorraine while the rest of us went off together.

That play opens with a coffin in the background on stage and the main character singing "Don't Cry For Me, Argentina." Since Lorraine had always been very fond of this song, it certainly touched our emotions. A little further along in the play, Eva Perron is shown going to her bed since she has cancer; we were all visibly moved, but perhaps that was a good outlet for us all.

We returned home to tell Lorraine about the excellent performance, decided we were all hungry and would order pizza. Lorraine wanted her share, and we will remember, all of us who had attended "Evita," standing around her bed enjoying our pizza with her. At one time she had told us it would be "die or diet," and since she always did enjoy her food, it was good that she never lost her appetite.

It was about this time that Lynn mentioned how her father, now living with the mother at Lynn Valley in Kiwanis Manor, had been helped a lot by therapeutic touch treatments. We were able to arrange for this special person to come to help Lorraine. Marlene worked with eliminating the negative somehow and Lorraine benefitted from these treatments. I had felt so positive because of Lorraine's life line, but she said to Larry she wished I wouldn't look through rose-colored glasses. When I went back to Victoria and read up in the Cheiro's book I found that long line did not always mean long life if there were other marks on the hand nearby. Whenever I phoned her I did remember to tell her I loved her. Somehow we need to do more of this when we are with members of our immediate family.

George had been out for a visit with his mother and she felt positive until he spoke of leaving. On August 6th I recorded "...but tonight she had morphine -- has a walker now beside the commode chair and seems to have given up."

"Today at noon she stopped all the herbs! But she is still eating."

Arlene and I alternated with being in North Vancouver or in Victoria. Larry's parents came to stay for a few days. Son John visited with his girl friend; Laverne and her fellow called often. Lynn took over with the neck rubbing when we were not there. One night when she couldn't sleep Larry phoned Michael Judd. Although he had never tried it before, he gave Larry instructions over the phone which resulted in Lorraine falling into a sound sleep. Michael returned to the house in person the next day to reinforce the instructions. The morphine dose was increased by the doctor and a stronger type was also ordered.

George came out again bringing his young son with him -- he had been given compassionate leave. It was on the 13th that we went to see Evita and the next day that the family went on shifts so that somebody was always with Lorraine. Max and daughter Louise arrived on the 16th so I made sure I was in Victoria that day.

On the morning of the 17th Lorraine awakened and asked what the date was. She then lapsed into a coma, and when they woke her up for the morphine shot told them that wasn't needed as it had been so beautiful where she was. They did not wake her again. I received a phone call to come over on the ferry, and another one when I was on the ferry. She had been in a coma for 8 hours before she made her transition. Although I hugged her when I came in the door I could see she was no longer there, and it did not take me long to swallow some vodka on the rocks. I apparently had two of these. The write up for Saturday the 17th shows I was under the influence.

Max was sleeping outside on a sleeping bag and according to Louise, I wrote "Grandpa is in the fetal position wishing for the mother he never had and the father he never was." Marlene told us how she had never been in a situation where there was so much love. Her words were "I've never seen a more loving family."

On Monday afternoon Larry called me into the bedroom: "Zanzara, Zanzara, come quick". He had had an incredible experience, "Lorraine was just here." Ming who had never let her be alone, had jumped up and been sniffing the air.

Before the different family members left their homes, we had all Lorraine's friends come to the house. One of the friends she and Larry had worked with made all of the refreshments. There was no funeral since one of the promises made was that her ashes go to Maui. Another promise I had made Lorraine was that I would go to see David Young with Laverne. Lorraine and I had been to him several years previously and knew he was an excellent medium.

Laverne and I made that promised visit to David Young on October 12th -- not quite two months later. David knew somehow that she had not been buried and he was quite surprised that she was back so soon. Through David, Lorraine had much to say. First she did not like my hair and said I looked like a sergeant major. (She never did like me with straight hair.) Then she did not like the beads Laverne was wearing over a T shirt and told her she should wear them with a green dress, which really was true! She liked Laverne's hair at its length and told her to keep it that way. Then she enquired about Laverne's boy friend as to how they were getting along and reminded her that there were lots more fish in the sea.

Laverne did not understand the "Who's doing the cooking?" question so I reminded her that her

60

mother wanted to know who had taken over her cooking position. Laverne was then able to tell who had, and as it happened that was the very person Lorraine had hoped would get the job. Many questions could only have been asked by Lorraine so we knew she had to be there in a spirit form. She wanted "lover boy" to take her ashes over to Maui -- he was to travel first class and "drink his face off." (These two expressions were new to me but familiar to my sister.) She wanted to know if we had given away the rest of her clothes and of course we had done just that. (Her sister took them home, which was very fitting.)

In a comment about her son John, she said "We will never get him married, but what's the sense in getting married just for the sake of being married. Right, Mom?"

I am sure Lorraine was met by our parents in her transition as both were there that day with her. It must have a very joyous reunion for them to be with their first grand-daughter once again.

Lorraine's big concern was the house Arlene and I were buying in Maui. She did not want it to become a mausoleum, and made numerous suggestions about our selling the house and buying a condo, either down in Lahaina near the airport or even over in Honolulu.

Once I think she must have used her favorite four letter word and David almost blushed and commented "Oh I couldn't say that". Next he sheepishly came up after bending down low and said "What's this -- tell lover boy to get his ass in gear."

Her final comment was one of the most interesting:

"We make all these promises beforehand, and afterwards it doesn't matter; the ashes can go anywhere."

Arlene and I lost two first cousins that very month, within two weeks of each other, and the two of us decided if we were ever going to enjoy the house in Hawaii we had better get over there as soon as possible. The car we had sent over had been left in the double garage when we had returned in June of that year. We felt the house never did become a mausoleum.

Soon after we had gone over in November, Larry made the promised trip with her ashes. He broke down at the airport as it was the first time Lorraine wasn't there to meet him, but he told us he had seen her in the clouds when he left Honolulu for Maui.

Her ashes stayed with us in the house for quite a long time as Larry had thought one of her sons should be with him for the scattering. I remember one time he rolled the container down the hall saying, "All right, go to bed early if you want to!" She was always into bed very early. It was February of the next year that Arlene and I went with him on the trip to Makena Beach. Shortly after Larry walked out into the water with the container, a breeze got up and in the scattering, some of the ashes went up his nose. He was sure she had the last laugh then — perhaps she was getting even for the time he rolled the container down the hall.

Unknown to each other, Lorraine's oldest niece from Masset, B.C. and Lynn's daughter both wrote a composition about Lorraine. Both reports received high ratings. Here is the one from Lynn's daughter.

Progress Report No. 1

During the summer I experienced a very tragic death. I learned a great deal from this and it has benefitted me greatly. Through this, I learned how to cope with death, I have learned how to become more involved with myself spiritually, also I have experienced the loss of a loved one. This has affected my outlook on life dearly.

In the past I was scared of death, people close to death, or even seeing death. The lady who lived downstairs from us and her husband (Lorraine and Larry), had been battling cancer for about six months. Lorraine had a masectomy about five years ago. Early last February Lorraine found out that she had a brain tumor and had a few months to live. In her last couple of months we saw her health deteriorate rapidly. She stayed in bed constantly, soon needed to wear diapers and to be fed through a straw. Every day I would go down and visit her and help her in any way I could. It was very hard and soon I faced reality -- not totally until the end.

During Lorraine's last weeks, she and Larry went to Hawaii and got married. They also became very involved in past-life regression, self-hypnosis and spiritual beings. Through this I learned a great deal about the different spiritual beings and about myself, spiritually. Larry knew how to relax you through a type of hypnosis. It was a unique experience and I enjoyed it thoroughly.

The last couple of days of Lorraine's life were terrible. She was right out of it. On Saturday, August 17, I came home from work and Lorraine was in a coma. (We kept her at home until she died.) I sat with her all night and it was the best and worst experience. During that time, seeing her die and sitting with her after she died was very traumatic and heart-breaking. The long term effects have helped me and I know I can cope, understand, and relate to death better.

The conclusion: I feel that this experience has benefitted me both in my favor and not in my favor. I still feel the pain of the loss but I have a greater understanding of myself, the world spiritually and environmentally, and to others around me. For I will be able to share my experiences with others to hopefully help them.

Lorraine's niece a thousand miles away wrote the following, which was headed "Based on a True Story."

Return to Onelea Beach

The sudden phone call from Vancouver stunned the whole family. It was my aunt, my mother's older and only sibling. It sounded so final — cancer. It was ironic. She had always complained that her breasts were too large and heavy and now the doctors were going to take one away from her. Cancer always happens to the other person, not somebody close to you. It didn't seem fair. In some ways being a close family has its disadvantages. When one of your relatives hurts, you hurt right along with them.

Lorraine always believed she would die young, but when faced with the near possibility of death I guess she must have changed her mind. She fought her damnest to beat the disease.

My aunt could do some weird things. She had some form of ESP; she could tell when the phone would ring and who it would probably be. This happened a lot whenever my mother or her mother would phone her. I found it to be unreal. Lorraine also strongly believed in reincarnation, which helped her to better understand her life a few years later.

Yes, a few years later, my aunt beat the cancer and we thought it was all over, but the worst was yet to come. I know why she beat the cancer, but first, I should explain how she acquired it.

You see my Aunt had never really been happy. She was constantly moving around during all her travels. She found that she was drawn to Maui and in particular, Onelea Beach, for some reason she couldn't explain. She had borne three children, all had different fathers. She seemed to be looking for someone that she couldn't find. And one day she found that somebody.

His name was Larry. Some call it fate; I know

that it had to have been planned. She was finally happy. For some strange reason Larry was also drawn to Maui, and the two of them were drawn to Onelea Beach.

In 1981, something went wrong and they split up. Lorraine fled to Maui. It was here that she detected the lump in her breast. The doctor ordered her back to Canada. She was later told that when the mind hurts, the body reacts in a bad way. We all believe that she brought the cancer on herself as she was so devastated about the break-up.

Just before her return to Vancouver, my Aunt had an out-of-the-body experience; she wouldn't tell me what it was about, said I was too young to understand. I just recently found out and now I understand. During her out-of-the-body experience she met Larry; he confessed to sharing a bottle of wine with a mutual friend of theirs and going to bed with her. Then Lorraine returned to Vancouver. She confronted Larry with that experience she'd had. He nearly died, his face went white. It was true. He had met Lorraine but had thought it was only a dream.

The lump in her breast turned out to be malignant, but they had caught it in time. She would be OK. It was during this time she and Larry reconciled.

Then last year in the Springtime it seemed to be happening again; it didn't seem fair. She was finally happy. Not again -- why her?

This time it was much more serious. She'd had some sort of epileptic attack and the doctors wanted her to have a CAT scan to determine the problem. The results of the scan were astonishing and incomprehensible. The verdict -- an inoperable malignant brain tumor. It seemed like a bad dream. Is this really happening?

Then she asked if she would be around for Christmas. The doctor said she'd be lucky if she would be around to see summer. He felt that she had three weeks left to live.

It was her wish that she spend her last few weeks in Maui. But before they left, she and Larry asked to see the scan. It showed two tumors and during the attack they had fused together as one.

Before they left, she gave away all her clothes. In her words, "People won't want to take my clothes after I'm dead." Soon after the results of the scan, Larry asked her to marry him. She was astonished as this had been her dream ever since her divorce from her last husband had been finalized. She promised him that she would will herself to stay well in order for them to be married in Hawaii.

Just before they left, my Aunt arranged with a hypnotist to have her previous lives revealed, as she believed in reincarnation. Because of her ESP power she was an excellent candidate for hypnosis. On the first visit the man doing the hypnosis explained to her that she could destroy the tumor with her mind. On the second visit, she went back into her past lives. There were many, but the most interesting one was where she had been born in the year 1800, living at Onealoa Beach. It was here that she met Larry. She left her husband and children for him. When she was 43, Larry left her and she experienced dreadful loneliness and unhappiness, much like the unhappiness she had during this lifetime.

This explained why she and Larry were fated to be together and why they both loved Maui so much.

So they flew to Maui and on June 4, 1985, were united as man and wife as it was meant to be. Lorraine proved the doctors wrong and she lived longer than they had said. I visited her in July and she seemed like the same Lorraine I knew and will always remember. But you could tell that the end was near. She kept telling me that my mother had to come down as soon as possible. In early August we received a phone call that my Aunt wanted my Mom and her father to come NOW. My Aunt waited until they arrived before she would leave. A lot of my rel-

66

atives have birthdays in August and she refused to die on one of these dates.

When asked when she would be back, and in what form, my Aunt replied, "I'm not coming back for a while, I'm too pissed off with this life."

On August 17, a day before her second son's birthday my Aunt passed away in her sleep, in my mother's arms.

A couple of months later her ashes were scattered on Onealea Beach.

Laverne once told me her mother had told her when she was young that she would only live to her middle forties. Lorraine was 46 years old the year she died. During those same years when Laverne and her mother were together, her mother often had headaches. These she would brush off as being her "brain tumor." One should be very wary about projecting adverse thoughts about health, because thoughts really are things. Often you can prove this to yourself if you have gone to get something and forget what it was you went for. When you return to where you made the decision you will collect that thought again.

Just when Lorraine and I had been together in another life will have to be in a second story, but it is programmed that we will be together again, though in just what roles will no doubt be decided in another dimension.

It took me a few years to accept her loss -- we had such fun times together when we did any traveling. She loved kicking in the leaves, and this Fall I have been reminded of her often whenever I walk among the leaves on the paths near our home. We are back living in Victoria, having completed the dream Lorraine had. One memorable comment she made won't be forgotten: she told us all of her dreams or wishes had been fulfilled, but she was dying. It is my hope that her next life will be a truly happy one.

This life is just a skein of time which we weave into a tapestry for our immortal souls. Time as we know it here does not exist this way in spirit realms.

Postscript

When Lorraine made her transition, you may remember that I went to see David Young as had been promised. Time passed by and Tamara's daughter was due to have her first baby. The baby was a girl and Louise asked her psychic sister if this could be "Auntie Lorraine" back again. The sister said "Yes, she is."

1993

It was that summer when this little girl, Latasha, was here with the aunt when the following happened. While the aunt was at the dentist's, I was looking after this great-granddaughter. I took her to the piano to have a Kelly Kirby Kindergarten piano lesson which begins with playing "Two black keys walking up." Suddenly she said, "Who's that?" about a picture of Lorraine I have on the piano when she was "dressed to the nines" for a trip to Paris. I said, "That's Auntie Lorraine." Then I took a small-framed picture I have of her at the side when she was young and said "And this is Auntie Lorraine when she was a little girl." Latasha said "That's me." (The goose bumps ran up and down my neck and head at this comment, but I said nothing to her.) At that time Latasha was three years old.

A few days later when the aunt was away once again for a dental appointment, I was at the piano once again with Latasha. We did the "two black keys walking up" and "baby middle C," etc. Then she said once again to me "Who's that?" I once again said "That's Auntie Lorraine," then I pointed to the other small-framed picture and said "And that's her when she was a little girl." Latasha said immediately, "She's looking at the ducks." Believe me then I really had those bumps again but said nothing. The thing is there are no ducks in that picture, but I have the snapshot of her when she was about that same age and is looking at the ducks at Beacon Hill Park. It is a picture I treasure and had thought I might paint sometime. There are no ducks in that small picture and daughter Lorraine is just sitting on a stump. I then knew that Auntie Carmen's comment was no doubt true and that Latasha is the soul representative sent this time for Lorraine.

We come here in different guises to learn lessons, and since she never liked the role of a woman, perhaps that is why she is again a female. Lately I have also wondered if she is here to find out what it is like to have half sisters and such, to experience what George, John and Laverne had to contend with in this lifetime after she went off with Larry. I suppose we will only find out how all these arrangements are made after we, too, are on the other side and it is decided what our next lessons will be.

Since there are quite a few people who have read *A Skein of Time* by Zanzara Hennigan, I felt I should run off a copy or two for these friends. Since dashing off this extra, another item surfaced. My great-granddaughter told me the family had been to Mom's for supper and Latasha made this comment, "I have to eat lots, so I'll be big and strong the way I used to be." Lorraine used to have two sets of clothes, her "fat ones" and those she wore after dieting. The tendency was for her to be big and strong.

Early in 1995 I painted the scene with the ducks at Beacon Hill Park for Latasha. Previous life memories do not occur anymore as she is now of school age. That was what I believed early in 1996, but another event occurred during a summer visit to Masset, when a second sister arrived for Latasha and so Zanzara Hennigan is adding a little more to this edition.

I had told Latasha and Victoria about the cat, "Ankhe" who had returned to us by a creek at Nass Camp, after having been gone for a long time. It was a day or two later that I was asked by Latasha about the painting I had given her mother. I told her it was the house we had had on Maui. Then I went on to explain I had signed the picture "Zanzara," but that I used to sign them "E.C.B." and "Your mother has one in the bathroom signed that way." So in we went to view the picture. It happens to be a watercolour I painted of a view from the teacherage.

I was able to show them where the creek was at the side of the picture and then pointed out "And there are the trailers where Auntie Vicky lived." "I know" said Latasha, matter of factly, "I've been there." Once again I had the goose bump experience at my neck and head but did not

70

make any comment to them. ("Vicky" became Lorraine in both of the books. I explain this in the book about the Nass.)

A few nights later I happend to notice that she had a large piece of meat that was half fat and half meat, and that she was eating it all with relish. Her appetite is still excellent, and of course the daughter who journeyed to the next dimension, always enjoyed her meat that way as well, and all her food. Latasha is now in Grade 1 and attended kindergarten all last year. I would like to be here to talk to her about all this when she is older.

Zanzara Hennigan, September, 1996